A National Trust Old Postcard Album

Geoffrey Sowerby

Foreword by the Marquess of Anglesey

The Pentland Press Ltd.
Edinburgh.Cambridge.Durham

First published in 1993 by
The Pentland Press Ltd.
Hutton Close
South Church
Durham
in association with The National Trust
(Enterprises) Ltd.

ISBN 1 872795 88 9

Produced in Great Britain by
Hillprint Ltd., Bishop Auckland

To
Madeleine

Acknowledgements

Iam indebted to many people with whom I have spoken or corresponded in connection with this book. They include the Marquess of Anglesey for so kindly agreeing to contribute a Foreword, Sir Richard Hyde-Parker, Bart., Brian Carter, Mrs D.Woolner, Mrs E.N. Sandford, Miss Rosamund Griffin, Sarah Kay, and the Administrator at Little Moreton Hall.

My thanks also to staff at Bath Central Library, Gloucestershire Record Office and Burton upon Trent Public Library; to Alex Youel (now National Trust Marketing Manager) and Kerry Usher (Administrator, Calke Abbey) whose co-operation made possible the original postcard displays at Calke which led to the assembling of this collection for publication; and to Mrs Rosalind Stonier for secretarial assistance.

I much appreciate the advice and assistance received over many months from Anthony Phillips and Daniel Russell of the Pentland Press Ltd., and also the co-operation of the National Trust with whom this book is published in association.

I am grateful for permission to use quotations from *Miss Clare Remembers* by 'Miss Read' (Michael Joseph Ltd.), and from H.V. Morton's books *In Search of England* and *In Search of London* (Methuen).

The postcards are from my own collection but I think we should all acknowledge the many photographers and publishers, known and unknown, who produced these splendid scenes in the golden age of the picture postcard.

G.H.S.

Foreword

by the Marquess of Anglesey DL FSA FRHistSHon FRIBA FRSL

Those alluring records described in the *Shorter Oxford Dictionary* as 'pasteboard cards of a regulation size, bearing a picture on the reverse side, used for correspondence', are collectors' items of real importance to an understanding of the physical shape of the nation's past and present. This is especially so where the built heritage is concerned. They are of equal interest when they illustrate how the countryside, natural and man-made, appeared in years gone by.

The collection of old picture postcards gathered together here by Geoffrey Sowerby is a captivating and instructive register of what National Trust properties looked like from the dawn of photography. The earliest is a calotype taken by William Henry Fox Talbot of Lacock Abbey, dated 1842. Most of the rest date from the earlier part of this century.

Numbers of them have proved of considerable value when the Trust came to acquire the properties which they portray. To know, for instance, what a more or less derelict garden looked like in its previous owner's time is of practical importance when a reconstruction of it is to be made. The same often applies to the exteriors and interiors of country houses and other historic buildings.

Important though the utility of these visual chronicles is to the Trust, what makes this book particularly worthwhile, appealing and so tremendously enjoyable for the general viewer and reader is the feeling of pleasing nostalgia which they induce.

By themselves, of course, they can give considerable but only limited delectation, whereas with a commentary upon each of them, explaining something of the history of the places depicted and, where appropriate, telling anecdotes of the people who once owned them, they come to life most strikingly.

These verbal vignettes, pithy and to the point, tell us just enough to whet our appetites for more. They remind us what an amazing variety of outstanding properties is in the Trust's capable and sensitive hands, ranging from Alfriston Clergy House, the first building to be transferred to it, to the grandeurs of Knole, Kedleston and Blickling; from the splendours of its landscaped gardens, such as that at Studley Royal, to the rugged wildness of the Winnats and Mam Tor in Derbyshire; from the Bridge House in Cumbria and the Greyfriars, Worcester, to the little known Roman Bath in London, the triangular folly of Paxton's Tower in Dyfed and Plas Newydd in Anglesey where I am privileged still to live.

Geoffrey Sowerby has produced a truly enchanting album, a notable and very welcome addition to the burgeoning literature of that shiningly admirable institution the National Trust which has secured for posterity so much of Britain's heritage for the gratification of posterity.

Introduction

Compiling this album of old postcard views showing National Trust properties, as they were before coming into Trust ownership, was encouraged by the response of visitors at two exhibitions staged in Calke Abbey, Derbyshire, in 1986 and 1987. This fascinating house, then newly acquired, was opened over one weekend each year to allow the public to view progress on restoration; *The National Trust on Old Postcards* was displayed in the Library to provide added interest during the tour of otherwise empty rooms. My aim was to show the range and variety of Trust properties and changes in their appearance over the years. Postcards are an appropriate medium for this purpose because both the National Trust and picture postcards share the same birthday and their stories thus advance side by side

When the National Trust was inaugurated at a small gathering convened on 16 July 1894, it took as its full title, 'The National Trust for Places of Historic Interest and Natural Beauty'. In the same year, George Stewart & Company of Edinburgh and F.T. Corkett of Leicester are generally credited with producing the first true British picture postcards, but scores of firms all over the country were soon publishing view-cards, many of them showing 'places of historic interest and natural beauty'. These early postcards were mainly contemporary photographs recording places as they were long before anyone could have realised that one day many of them would become properties of the infant National Trust.

The history of the picture postcard is a story of rapid growth and popularity with an almost immediate 'golden age'; by 1914 around 880 million cards were being posted every year. Growth of the National Trust was, by comparison, methodical but slow, and in terms of actual membership now seems hardly spectacular with 250 members in 1900 and 8,000 by 1935. Membership expansion only really began when many more properties, particularly country houses, were being opened to the public after the Second World War, the total reaching 23,000 in 1950 and 97,000 in 1960. Costwise, the National Trust subscription of 10 shillings (50p), agreed in 1895, stayed unchanged until 1953. The postal charge of one halfpenny to send a postcard remained in force until June 1918 when the rate was increased to one penny.

Not only do old postcards - now being enthusiastically collected for the second time - show present-day Trust properties as they appeared between sixty and one hundred years ago; reproductions of prints or engravings often contribute an unusual historical record of an old site or building. The value of postcards as source material for local, social, historical and architectural records is now widely acknowledged. In some cases the written message, which from 1902, no longer had to share the picture side of the card, can provide added interest when it chronicles a visit to the place shown or is written from it or about it. It is, of course, a National Trust property which has the distinction of featuring on the world's oldest surviving photographic negative - Fox Talbot's 1835 view of an oriel window at Lacock Abbey.

Some postcards are delightful miniature works of art in their own right as many accomplished artists found an outlet for their talents, publishers offering high quality reproductions of their paintings and commissioning sets of cards. Knole, for example, was extensively portrayed through sets of original paintings published as postcards early in the century.

Although the 'souvenir' postcard was an early innovation, many of these old cards were of places senders or recipients never actually visited. This applied particularly to country houses which often remained strictly private except, perhaps, on special occasions when local people might visit the grounds for fêtes, a meet of hounds or an event such as a Coronation celebration or an heir's coming of age. Enterprising photographers were usually there to record the occasion, and in a period when few newspapers carried any pictures - often of poor quality when they did - it was postcards that people bought to keep as a memento or to send to friends. They would be on sale within a day or two of the event.

Some houses and castles have, of course, long been open to visitors at certain times. Publicity for this, and comments and reactions of visitors, make an interesting social study in themselves. Postcards on public sale were generally of exterior views. Found less frequently are interior scenes, of much interest today since these often show greater changes than outside scenes, as well as recording the original furnishing and arrangements of rooms; garden scenes too, illustrate changing design over the years.

In any thematic postcard collection there will be certain 'fringe' card which have such a close connection with the topic that they seem to qualify for consideration. This selection does contain two or three such items and while they do not depict actual National Trust properties, their significance seemed fully to justify inclusion in this album. Hopefully, the text will explain their presence.

This volume is in no way intended as a guide book. The period scenes featured are the popular views of early this century of places destined to become today's preserved buildings and protected localities, collectively attracting millions of visitors. The brief text aims, whenever possible, to illustrate the view with a little of the more unusual information to be gleaned from sources contemporary with, or earlier than the cards - obsolete guidebooks, notes by early visitors, comments from the cards themselves - and to record the developing story both of picture postcards and of the National Trust.

Today these once humble little items from the pages of old family albums have a new appeal, interest and social history value, as well as providing a nostalgic glimpse from the past of places whose future is now secured for our enjoyment.

LACOCK ABBEY
Wiltshire

Lacock Abbey: Home of Fox-Talbot.   From an original made by Fox-Talbot, in 1842.

The Introduction mentioned the world's oldest photographic negative showing a window at Lacock. It was produced by William Henry Fox Talbot in August 1835 as the first successful printing of a photograph on paper, a process which Fox Talbot patented as 'calotype'. It permitted any number of copies to be made from one negative, introducing the negative/positive principle of modern photography, so that the subsequent story of the picture postcard can be said to have had its beginnings here also.

The postcard shown reproduces an original Fox Talbot photograph of 1842. His invaluable early work miraculously escaped the 'tidying up and turning out' which has so often led to the loss of priceless records and it was presented to the Science Museum by the photographer's granddaughter, Miss Matilda Talbot, who later gave the house to the National Trust in 1944.

Lacock incorporates monastic remains, adapted to form a Tudor mansion with eighteenth-century 'Gothick' alterations following later. The sixteenth-century tithe barn has been converted to house the Fox Talbot Photographic Museum, telling the story of his life and work, and the estate village is also under Trust ownership.

THE OLD POST OFFICE, TINTAGEL
Cornwall

An early National Trust acquisition (1903), this fourteenth-century stone manor house was rescued and restored as one of the few surviving examples in south-west Britain of a domestic dwelling of the Middle Ages, an antiquity perhaps tending to be obscured by its being known as the Old Post Office. It has been refurbished as such although this usage only covers the period from 1844 to 1892. During that time it no doubt handled many early plain postcards but its closure came before the advent of Britain's first picture postcards in 1894.

The world's first postcard was issued in Austria on October 1st.1869, the first British cards following exactly one year later. These were plain cards with an embossed stamp obtainable only from post offices and selling at one halfpenny each. Subsequently they had to be bought in dozens for 6½ old pence. This followed complaints from the stationery trade that the Post Office monopoly represented unfair competition in that the cost of the card was included with the cost of the stamp. About 150 million were sold within the first two years, foreshadowing the later enthusiasm for picture postcards.By 1914 these were being posted at the rate of over 850 million a year.

COURT CARD (actual size) CLUMBER
Nottinghamshire

This is a good example of an early court size card. It was produced by one of the most prolific of postcard publishers, Valentines of Dundee, whose first cards appeared in 1897. It illustrates the limitations of court cards as a picture record, especially where more than one scene is depicted.

Worksop is on the fringe of the area known as the Dukeries and three of the mansions shown here were ducal properties. No one could then have imagined a day when Clumber would be a National Trust park, the famous lime avenue a public road, and the stables - once full of horses and carriages - a Trust regional headquarters. The house, top left, was demolished in 1938 but G.F. Bodley's High Victorian Gothic chapel has been fully restored.

At the time of the postcard, Clumber House might be 'shown during the absence of the family' and permission to drive through the park could be obtained from certain local hotels where conveyances were available for hire.

BLICKLING HALL
Norfolk

Blickling Hall (II), near Aylsham

With all Kind Thoughts and Best Wishes for Christmas.

At the Annual General Meeting of the National Trust in 1934, Lord Lothian made a notable speech emphasising how social and economic pressures were drastically affecting the role and future of country houses. He urged the Trust to recognise the importance of preserving both houses and their contents. By new legislation the 'Country Houses Scheme' was eventually devised and Blickling, owned by Lord Lothian, was transferred to the Trust under its provisions in 1942.

At first sight the view (1902) may seem little different from that which hundreds of visitors photograph today, but it actually depicts the far more elaborate formal parterre garden with innumerable small beds, borders and topiary work, as laid out in 1872 and which, we are told, required an army of old age pensioners for its maintenance. It was greatly simplified to its present arrangement in 1930.

Visitors are nothing new at Blickling, however, and it was open to fashionable tourists in the later eighteenth century. Lady Beauchamp Proctor, writing in 1772, described how 'We saw only the old part of the house over which a very dirty housemaid with a duster in her hand, conducted us.'

This is an example of an early card with 'undivided back' which could carry only the address. The message space below the picture has been formally printed on this occasion to utilise an ordinary postcard for Christmas greetings.

GEORGE STEPHENSON'S COTTAGE
Northumberland

A scene to emphasise the range of properties in Trust ownership, this cottage at Wylam-on-Tyne was Stephenson's birthplace on 9 June 1781. He was the second of Robert Stephenson's six children; the family lived in two rooms until George was eight, three other families sharing the rest of the cottage. The menfolk were employed at Wylam colliery, and a wooden tramway serving it ran past the front door. Wylam's colliery days are now over but for long after Stephenson's time this was a typical Industrial Revolution landscape.

The postcard of *c.*1901 shows the cottage little altered from its original appearance and with family laundry hanging on the fence alongside what had become a main line of the North Eastern Railway. Today even that has gone, leaving the house in rural seclusion near the river and approached by a footpath, half a mile from Wylam which is now a pleasant residential village.

This is another 'undivided back' postcard but with the space for the message placed vertically to keep the best possible perspective for the picture. Notice the message as a good example of same day writing and posting (11.05am) with confidence in prompt delivery, locally almost certainly within an hour or two.

ALFRISTON CLERGY HOUSE
Sussex

The Old Parsonage — Alfriston

This was the first building to be purchased by the National Trust. Where today we think in terms of millions of pounds to restore and ensure preservation, this ancient priest's house was bought in 1896 for £10 when it was in ruinous condition and divided into two cottages. For once Trust ownership precedes the early postcard view which shows the newly thatched roof completing the restoration. A public appeal for £350 had been launched and this amount was eventually forthcoming with the help of the first grant from Trust funds.

The house itself dates from *c.*1350, and some architectural refinements inside suggest that it may originally have been supported by wealthy patronage. Its several rooms and outbuildings may also have provided accommodation for travellers whom medieval priests were required to receive, the poor paying nothing, the rest a moderate donation. Whatever the history of the house may be, it retains a very special place in the annals of the National Trust.

BARRINGTON COURT
Somerset

BARRINGTON COURT, SOM.

On a very different scale was the first large country house acquired by the Trust, in 1907 at a time when it was ill-equipped to deal with this sort of property. There was no endowment or provision for its maintenance. Montacute, in 1931, was the only other large house to come into Trust ownership prior to World War II and the Country Houses Scheme.

It was necessary for Barrington to be leased and initially little could be done other than making it weatherproof. It had been sadly treated with the interior largely gutted and the main staircase removed. Until after the First World War it continued in use as a farmhouse and the postcard clearly shows the sorry state it was in at this time; it could well be the farmer and his family who have posed for this photograph. A remarkable renovation of both house and garden was then undertaken by Colonel Lyle. He brought in Tudor and Jacobean panelling, installed a new grand staircase and even re-created a complete new room of *c*.1520 removed from a house in King's Lynn.

Some visitors have been critical of the use of Barrington Court as showrooms for a company making reproduction furniture and fittings but there needs to be sympathetic understanding of the background to the modern history of this lovely house, dating from the period 1514-20, and rescued by generous financial aid and devoted restoration work.

CORFE CASTLE
Dorset

Described up to the time of the Commonwealth as one of the most impregnable fortresses in the kingdom, this may explain why, in 1646, Corfe Castle was demolished far more extensively than was necessary to ensure that it became unusable as a military stronghold, so that it stands today as a spectacular but sadly mutilated ruin.

Perhaps unique for a National Trust property is a reference from pre-Conquest days when the Anglo-Saxon Chronicle records for the year 978:

'This year was King Edward slain at eventide at Corfe-gate, on the fifteenth day before the calends of April... No worse deed than this was ever done by the English nation since they first sought the land of Britain.'

The great enthusiasm for collecting picture postcards early this century led to many publishers reproducing old prints, etchings and paintings which, for many people, would be a first opportunity to see a familiar scene as it looked in past times. A ground plan of Corfe was drawn during a survey made in 1586 and this view is of a re-creation based on that plan. It gives a very fair impression of how awe-inspiring the castle must have looked to visitors approaching four hundred years ago.

BRAMBER CASTLE
West Sussex

Ruins of Bramber Castle, Sussex

Bramber is one of the few castles and National Trust properties to have a mention in the Domesday Book. It may well have been then a newly built structure, guarding the valley of the River Adur for the purpose of preventing any possible repetition of the Conqueror's own landing in the area. In the care of English Heritage it stands within a 12 acre Trust site below the South Downs. Greatly ruined, it had an early stone-built keep of considerable strength but not much is recorded of its history and destruction. The grounds, with fine views, have been a pleasure resort for some time.

This late Edwardian card shows a goodly number of visitors although there used to be an admission charge of one penny. It became a Trust property in 1946.

GLYN CEIRIOG
Clwyd

Glynceiriog Station.

One of the lost 'little railways' of Wales, the Glyn Valley Tramway was built in 1872-3 to serve slate and granite quarries near Glyn Ceiriog. An 8-mile single line of 2 ft. 4¼ ins gauge, ran from a wharf on the Shropshire Union Canal at Preesgweene from 1873, worked by horses after the trucks had descended by gravity as far as Pontfaen, the duty horse riding over this section in a rear wagon. The track then continued up the wooded valley through Castle Mill, Pontfadog, where there was a passing loop, and Dolywern to the station shown here at Glyn Ceiriog with its miniature platform, made after a passenger service was introduced.

The line was relaid half an inch wider extended to the Great Western Railway station and the canal at Chirk, and was converted to steam. Three engines worked freight and passenger trains, a fourth joining them in 1921, but competition from road services finally led to the end of passenger traffic in 1933 and the line was closed completely in 1935. Today the Trust owns meadowland and part of a public walk along the old trackway.

HINDHEAD COMMONS
Surrey

Hindhead, Punch Bowl, The Broom Squire's Cottage.

The Devil's Punch Bowl forms part of an extensive open area owned by the Trust around Hindhead. Much of it was an early acquisition from the Hindhead Preservation Committee in 1906 when it was actually under threat as a 'desirable site for residential development.' The 'Broom Squire' depicted may have been among the last of those traditional craftsmen who made birch brooms as their chief livelihood, but here he is carrying full, open pails of milk. This was a normal way of both collection and distribution at this time, a yoke balancing and spreading the weight.

The card is one of Francis Frith's splendid social history photographs of *c.*1907. The name 'Broom Squires' refers to broom squarers or broom makers. They worked in the Bowl until after the First World War and once practised an old country custom of hanging garlands of birch outside a cottage to keep demons away.

BERKHAMSTED COMMON
Hertfordshire

A peaceful pastoral scene but behind this photograph is the story of a great conservation battle fought some thirty years before the National Trust came into being. In 1866 the Commons Preservation Society elected to resist the enclosure of a substantial acreage of Berkhamsted Common by the forcible removal of fences. A special train conveyed 120 navvies, suitably equipped, to carry out this task peacefully and quietly. *Punch* described the reclamation in a long narrative poem, *A Lay Of Modern England*, proclaiming that 'our few remaining commons must not be seized or sold.'

Berkhamsted was the start of many successful campaigns which later led to the Trust becoming the guardians of many open spaces preserved as 'places of natural beauty.'

The postcard itself was published by W.H. Smith and is typical of the high quality photographic cards sold at their railway station bookstalls. Cards purchased on stations could often be posted straight away. It was not unusual for station postboxes to have up to twenty collections a day so that messages could be quickly dispatched for prompt delivery on the same day, thus: 'Calling in Rugby, expect me home tonight' on a card addressed to Stafford and postmarked Rugby Station.

WAGGONERS' WELLS
Hampshire

Waggoner's Wells, Hindhead

This picturesque area between Ludshott Common and Bramshott Chase was bought in 1919 following a public appeal and given as a memorial to Sir Robert Hunter, one of the Trust's founder members and solicitor to the Commons Preservation Society. Much early Trust activity was concentrated on the conservation of commons in Surrey, Sussex and Hampshire, and over 30,000 acres are now under Trust ownership.

Here, a series of hammerponds provided power for the Elizabethan iron industry. In the Civil War it was seen as a legitimate military target and destroyed by Cromwell. Later they were converted into fish-ponds and today the region is one of great natural beauty and interest throughout the year.

Very early in the century this young couple spread their picnic under the trees, but whether unexpectedly recorded for posterity or purposely posed by the photographer we shall probably never know.

ANTONY HOUSE
Cornwall

ANTONY. HOUSE   A.J.C

T he description of Antony as 'one of the most important and unspoilt Queen Anne houses in the West Country' could hardly have been applied at the time this view was photographed. It shows the unfortunate Victorian addition totally destroying the symmetry and overall appearance. It is a good example of a picture postcard record of a lost feature - a happy loss, in this case.

It was after The Second World War that architect Philip Tilden was called in to supervise a restoration. Somewhere nearby is an old quarry containing bricks from the demolition of the extension, buried there on the architect's strict instructions so that there should be no temptation to re-use them anywhere in the vicinity of this charming house, built in silver-grey Cornish stone.

LITTLE MORETON HALL
Cheshire

There is a cosy country cottage look about the kitchen of Little Moreton Hall as it was in Edwardian days, with a range built into the great medieval fireplace. At present this room is the National Trust shop, but door, window, and fireplace beam are immediately recognisable. Shop staff behind their small counter still stumble over the edge of the hearth which projects underneath the wall that blocked it up. From the garden can be seen the massive chimney stack which served it. Another item from this scene survives - the round table now stands in one of the window bays of the house.

The room adjoining the kitchen, used as a restaurant, was, at the time of this photograph, used as a dairy, and these former service rooms were entered from the screens passage which ran in the traditional manner across the end of the Great Hall.

Immediately after the second World War, Moreton Old Hall - as it was then usually designated-surely had what must be among the most extensive opening hours of any National Trust property - from March to October, including Sundays and Bank Holidays, from 9 am to 8 pm , and from 9 am to dusk from November to February, except for the first fortnight of November when the curator presumably took a well-earned, if out of season holiday. Admission was one shilling (5p), Children and Students, sixpence (2½p).

CALKE ABBEY
Derbyshire

W hen the National Trust acquired Calke in 1985 it received great publicity as a secret house revealed to the outside world for the first time. Given the family's love of privacy and that the house is nowhere viewable from any public road it is perhaps surprising that it was possible at least to see the exterior on a picture postcard. These were produced by 'Daddy' Martin, a typical local photographer from Melbourne who travelled around with his camera, tripod and equipment by bicycle, and made an extensive and high quality record of the surrounding area.

His card shows a feature removed early this century and which helps to explain a comment frequently made by today's visitors - that the main front entrance is rather insignificant for such a large mansion. Following the building of the house, in 1701-4, a wide flight of stone steps was erected in 1729 giving direct access to the Hall, now the Saloon.

When the portico was added, in 1806-8, these steps disappeared and were replaced by the iron staircases as recorded on the postcard. Their removal finally ended the original function of the Saloon as a grand entrance hall. These changes, with loss of foliage, have currently left a rather bare south front view, here relieved by the shrubs and floral displays in tubs and hanging baskets.

ANGLESEY ABBEY
Cambridgeshire

Like Calke Abbey, Anglesey was actually a priory which later 'promoted' itself. The postcard shows one of the many phases of its development into the treasure house it is today. When the main domestic quarters were created, the Jacobean south front was completed by dormer windows above the five bays. These were subsequently removed, giving the aspect recorded here. The careful restoration of the dormers then returned the house to its original appearance.

The photographer has introduced a little homely touch by including the young girl standing alongside the tennis net holding her sunhat.

CARLYLE'S HOUSE
London

Back of Carlyle's House from the Garden.

No. 24, Cheyne Row, Chelsea, dating from the early eighteenth century, was the home of the writer Thomas Carlyle from 1834 until his death in 1881. He rented it for £35 a year and wrote nearly all his works here. It is open today as a Carlyle museum containing personal relics and furniture, books and letters. There is a piano on which Chopin played, while another visitor was Lord Tennyson who recorded smoking a pipe with Carlyle at the kitchen fireside.

Commenting on this, *The Sketch* in December 1897 called attention to a pane of glass in the kitchen window engraved with the words: " 'John Herbert Knowles cleaned all the windows in this house and painted part in the 18 year of age, March 7th 1794.' This little record of a nonentity has been left undisturbed by the distinguished author." At the top of the house Carlyle had a room adapted in an unsuccessful attempt at sound proofing - so that he might be spared 'river and street noises and next door's cackling hens'.

It is interesting to find a postcard showing the plain rear view of the house including a rather drab London garden, but it was the associations of No. 24 which led to its acquisition by public subscription in 1895, making it a 'subject' for postcard souvenirs. It passed to the Trust in 1936.

COMPTON CASTLE
Devon

Almost contemporary with the postcard, the *Aldersgate Primitive Methodist Magazine*, 1904, offered its readers this descriptive visitors' guide: 'It is five miles from Torquay to Compton Castle - a desirable walk when you are in a contemplative mood. The way is by narrow and quiet lanes where you can botanize among an Eden of beauty, soliloquize until your speech startles you, and feast your eyes on ever varying landscapes of almost primitive loneliness ... Strictly speaking, the so-called castle is a fortified mansion and is said to be the finest building of the sort extant in England. It is grand in its ruins and affords many evidences of the habits and arrangements of feudal times ... The many ivy-covered gables give it a truly picturesque appearance.'

Visiting Compton today, especially in the holiday season, may be less idyllic but the 'picturesque ruin' presents a very different sight. Home of the Gilberts from the four-teenth century, the estate was sold in 1800 but repurchased in 1930 when the house was restored and the Great Hall rebuilt, so that it is now again a family home while still displaying its complete medieval layout.

DYRHAM PARK
Avon

W here today's National Trust visitors park their cars, Dyrham Park celebrated the Coronation of King George V and Queen Mary in June 1911. The festivities here would be typical of events held at big houses all over the country.

The sender of this card has marked it: 'R.W.B. in foreground.' This would be Robert Wynter Blathwayt of Dyrham Park who appears to be presiding over events and holding a starting pistol in his hand. Those spectators not attracted by the cameraman are probably following the progress of a race. 'Sports for all ages', even though competitors might remove only their best jackets, were a feature on occasions such as this when tenants and local inhabitants came together for fun and feasting.

An unusual aspect of the east front at Dyrham, well shown here, is the orangery attached to the house, left, with a balancing arcade running into the natural hillside on the right.

CLIVEDEN
Buckinghamshire

Cliveden Mansion. (South Front).

Here is one of the most beautiful parts of the river [Thames]. One slope is a mass of foliage for it supports the noted woods of Cliefden or Cliveden. The mansion to which this beautiful park belongs stands upon the plateau above and, as may be supposed, commands a view of surpassing beauty. A fire destroyed the old house and the present handsome structure was the work of Barry.

'In the old house the well-known air *Rule Britannia* is said to have been first heard here during the residency of Frederick, Prince of Wales, father of George III. The history of the house's destruction is another proof of how much mischief a foolish woman can do. One of the maid-servants was reading a novel in bed; the candle caught the curtains, and then, instead of extinguishing the flames, she fell down in a swoon. Before she could recover the fire had gained a head and burnt down the house.'

Such is the instructive and moral tale of Cliveden as found in the pages of a little girl's Sunday School prize in 1903, but a contemporary postcard message laments 'The Wesleyan Band of Hope, High Wycombe, used to go here for their annual outing when it belonged to the Duke of Westminster, but since it has been sold to Astor, the American millionaire, it has been closed to the public.'

In 1942 the 2nd Viscount gave Cliveden to the National Trust so that the extensive and beautiful grounds are again open. The house is let to a hotel group but three rooms may be viewed at certain times.

BRADLEY MANOR
Devon

W hen examining a postcard as a pictorial record, a need for caution has to be recognised. Many early cards were hand-coloured, sometimes with misleading results, of which Bradley provides an example. In one view, contemporary with this card, the artist has given the manor a red roof, suggesting that it was tiled. This was never the case although the Trust has carried out extensive restoration work on the roof, replacing Welsh slates with more authentic, graduated Cornish slates. This view clearly shows the Welsh slates and also the incongruous chimney-pots which were removed early in the century.

The east front of Bradley is now completely opened out, the wall here being a remnant of a period when the house was divided up in the nineteenth century. It was removed, along with the extension on the southern end of the range beyond it, when Cecil Firth, and later his daughter, Mrs Woolner, carried out an extensive restoration programme at this attractive old manor house.She gave the house to the Trust in 1938.

SMALLHYTHE PLACE
Kent

Small Hythe, nr. Tenterden, Ellen Terry's Farm. Frith

Here we have an example of a type of advertising postcard known as an 'insert'. Many periodicals, cheap paperback novels and romantic story magazines included free postcards with each issue. The view of Ellen Terry's house was among those issued with *Smart Novels*. This great and much loved actress bought Smallhythe in 1899 and lived there until her death in 1928. Born at Coventry in 1848 she had made her stage debut in 1856. Among her greatest triumphs were her performances as leading lady to Henry Irving.

The house, dating back to the fifteenth and sixteenth centuries, is now a memorial to Ellen Terry, and the Lyceum Room is a museum of this noted theatrical partnership. As well as costumes, playbills, properties and other theatrical memorabilia, there are exhibits and portraits from the careers of other distinguished players. Until the seventeenth century when the sea was receding and channels were silting up, Smallhythe was known as the Port House and adjoined a small shipyard.

'MISS ELLEN TERRY'S COTTAGE'

Within a short time of Ellen Terry establishing herself at Smallhythe, admirers were able to purchase photographic postcards showing much of the interior of the house as well as outside views. This card is one of several of *c.*1903 which record the original furnishing, and one aspect of these scenes is the almost complete absence of theatrical material. This personal touch has been retained in respect of today's arrangement of the bedroom - in contrast to most of the other rooms which are now largely of theatrical interest.

An actual photograph of an actress's bedroom was quite innovative at this time even if the caption was discreetly worded. Much of the furnishing of this room is unchanged. The double school desk was used by Ellen Terry's own children.

MELFORD HALL
Suffolk

This scene illustrates two aspects of country house life. During both World Wars mansions were commandeered for a variety of purposes and many never returned to being private residences. Of hundreds of houses demolished many were lost as a direct consequence of neglect and damage in the war years. Some were lost during their actual period of wartime usage, often through fire. Melford Hall was one of the lucky survivors though the north wing was gutted during military occupation in 1942. Happily, in this case, full restoration was carried out after the war and Melford came into the care of the National Trust in 1960.

The view is of added interest in that the little boy on the pony, William Stephen Hyde Parker, was to become the 11th Baronet and be responsible for restoring the north wing in front of which he is posed here with his uncle, Lawrence Hyde Parker. He was six years old at the time this photograph was taken in May 1898, and his son, the present Baronet, Sir Richard Hyde Parker, was able to trace the original photograph in the family album, finding details recorded on the back. It makes this a good example of a picture postcard subsequently produced from an earlier family photograph; and also demonstrates the value of recording information for future reference.

ANGLESEY CASTLE (PLAS NEWYDD)
Gwynedd

No house named Anglesey Castle appears in the National Trust guide. The postcard dates from early in the century when Plas Newydd had its name changed by the eccentric 5th Marquess of Anglesey, holder of the title from 1898 to 1905.

With an obsession for theatricals the Marquess had the Gaiety Theatre built in the Art Nouveau style in the former chapel. He established his own company, reserving leading roles for himself. Earlier he had specialised in *tableaux vivants* in which he appeared solo, dancing in lavish and exotic costumes and wearing rich jewellery from his enormous and valuable collection.

For his own theatre and 'provincial tours' he engaged the Anglesey Castle Orchestra. They were resident in the house for some time, playing also for spectacular fancy dress balls at which the Marquess awarded extravagant prizes. He squandered his personal fortune and after his death traces and records of the 'black sheep' at the 'castle' were swept away. It quickly reverted to its original name but some photographs and elaborate souvenir programmes are now on display at Plas Newydd.

OXBURGH HALL
Norfolk

T he late Dowager Lady Bedingfield, who died in 1985, would have been 102 on the day of her burial. She had lived through all the developments and patterns of change outlined in this book, growing up before the picture postcard became a new and exciting novelty and the National Trust was unheard of. When she came to Oxburgh as a young bride in 1904, the event was recorded as a happy social occasion at a time when country house life was at its zenith.

'A charming addition to the great Norfolk hostesses' reported *The Sketch*. 'Sir Henry and Lady Bedingfield are the fortunate owners of Oxburgh ... described as the finest example of brick architecture in the kingdom.'

Sir Henry died in 1941 and ten years later problems of maintenance and taxation obliged the sale of the property. There was a real threat of demolition when Lady Bedingfield repurchased the hall and, with the aid of various trust funds, was able to transfer it to the National Trust.

The postcard can be dated to within a year or two of Lady Bedingfield becoming mistress of Oxburgh and shows the old arrangement of the King's Room in the splendid fifteenth-century gatehouse which escaped the extensive Victorian Gothic alterations to the hall. The Mary Queen of Scots and Elizabeth Shrewsbury bed and wall hangings are now displayed elsewhere in the house under conservation conditions.

LYME PARK
Cheshire

Most photographs of Lyme Park concentrate on Leoni's imposing Palladian south front and the terraced gardens and ornamental lake. This postcard captures much of the natural setting for this great house amid wild moorland and with the hills still rising up beyond the house, the estate standing higher than almost any other in the country. This scene is also a reminder that there was a grand house here in the sixteenth century. While the drawing room and long gallery are internal reminders, it is only this north front that retains external evidence, with its fine tall Tudor gateway entrance to the central courtyard.

GREAT CHALFIELD MANOR
Wiltshire

Chalfield Manor.

While the north façade of Great Chalfield remains today as built in 1480, much has happened behind it. Fortunately, drawings of the manor were made in 1836 when, although becoming very dilapidated, the house was still virtually intact and these survived to assist a careful and sympathetic reconstruction and restoration made from 1905 to 1913. Soon after the record of 1836 the east wing was demolished and subsequently much of the west wing collapsed.

This postcard scene pre-dates the start of restoration and clearly shows the west oriel window open to the elements and the wing unroofed. The foreground has also been much changed with a new entrance archway built. The man with his smock and yoke is a reminder of how the old house had virtually been reduced to mere farm outbuildings.

The small adjoining church was added to by Thomas Tropnell who had built Chalfield and his mural portrait, which survives in the unique dining-room adjoining the Great Hall, represents the earliest known picture of a Member of Parliament. This classic example of changes in domestic architectural styles which characterised the fifteenth century, came to the National Trust in 1943.

TRERICE
Cornwall

D ating from the sixteenth century, this is another Trust property which has survived a period of considerable neglect, becoming a farmhouse and then being partially ruined when the gable of the north wing blew down.

This pre-First World War postcard shows an overgrown garden, the foliage almost hiding the derelict north wing, right, as well as nearly concealing the fine 24 light window of the Great Hall with its 576 panes of glass. Trerice was fully renovated in 1954-55, when the north wing and gable were reconstructed; after considerable clearance, the very interesting garden was also carefully restored and redesigned.

DUNHAM MASSEY
Cheshire

The Hall, Dunham Park.

TAKEN BY "THE RAJAR SYSTEM" OF PHOTOGRAPHY

When the 9th Earl of Stamford took up residence at Dunham in 1909 he found the hall in rather a sorry condition. He not only put in hand alterations and redecoration inside but instituted extensive changes to the south entrance front of the house.

A photograph from this point today shows a much altered façade, the plain entrance bay made much more elaborate and the roof lines changed to give dormer windows to the second and fourth bays.

The card, postmarked 1904, is thus a record of the south front prior to this restoration. It was produced by the quaintly named 'Rajah' system of photography from the Brooks-Watson Daylight Camera Company of Liverpool and Mobberley.

WIGHTWICK MANOR
West Midlands

Photo by A. B. Hart   Wightwick Manor. Wolverhampton   Wolverhampton

There can be few postcard collectors who, at one time or another, have not been frustrated and disappointed to hear of old family albums thrown away or destroyed on bonfires because 'we didn't think they would ever be of interest to anyone'. Items belonging to fairly recent times are often unappreciated until too late and are more liable to be disposed of than things from earlier periods.

A similar dilemma undoubtedly faced the National Trust when it was offered Wightwick Manor on the outskirts of Wolverhampton in 1937, a time when the Trust owned very few large houses. Wightwick had been built only fifty years before and might have seemed hardly to fit the Trust's commitment to 'Places of Historic Interest'.

Fortunately, encouraged by expert opinions, it was accepted and this splendid monument to the Pre-Raphaelite Movement was preserved intact with its tapestries and wallpapers by William Morris, glass by Kempe, decorative tiles by De Morgan, and many other contemporary works of art, drawings and paintings. The garden was designed by the painter Alfred Parsons RA.

STOURHEAD
Wiltshire

Multi-view cards were very popular in Edwardian days and are found with many variations of shapes and designs forming a group of small pictures. The idea developed from the Continent, particularly Germany, where, from the 1880s, most places already has their local cards inscribed *GRUSS AUS* [Greetings from] as used on this Stourhead souvenir of *c.*1904. Each scene was generally available as a single postcard or forming a set and sold in a paper envelope.

This card concentrates on the famous gardens which have long attracted visitors. Stourhead mansion, one of the first Palladian houses to be built in Britain, was completed in 1724 and it was Henry Hoare II who began work on the pleasure grounds in the 1740s. Enjoying them today we might reflect on the imagination and planning that went into their creation - damming to form the lake, immense earth moving, siting and planting of trees, quarrying and transport of stone, together with the building of the grotto, temples and bridges.

Pausing to admire it all, as so many do every year, we can surely sympathise with an American, Louis Simond, who, early last century, sat down in the mansion to admire a picture and was told that it was 'the rule of the house not to allow visitors to sit down'.

WESTBURY COURT GARDENS
Gloucestershire

In 1967 when the Trust took over the derelict water garden at Westbury, the restoration of canals, pavilion and garden seemed an ambitious and daunting undertaking, perhaps surpassed in scale only by the project at Biddulph.

Westbury was a survival of an early formal garden of 1697-1705 which escaped the later fashion for landscaping. The house, the third Westbury Court to stand on the site, was demolished in 1961, leaving silted canals, dead hedges, crumbling walls and a garden which had returned to nature.

The postcard view of the long canal belongs to the period before decline set in but it also shows how the Dutch-style pavilion had lost its identity when incorporated into the house.

PETWORTH HOUSE
West Sussex

Petworth House, the seat of Lord Leconfield, is a rather plain mansion, reconstructed by Charles, Duke of Somerset. There is a chapel, part of the old mansion, ornamented with arms and badges. The house contains a magnificent collection of pictures by old and modern masters ; a sculpture gallery with many antique statues and busts, and there is a fine collection

of exquisite carvings. A sword stated to have been used at the battle of Shrewsbury is in the house. The park, containing many noble trees and affording views of beauty and grandeur, is 10 miles in circumference.

PETWORTH HOUSE

Adding of information to a postcard of a country house was not a wide practice. This is perhaps understandable when most houses were still privately owned before World War II and comparatively few of them were open to the public.

The publicity card for Petworth is something of a novelty, being an aerial view taken between the wars by Surrey Flying Services of Croydon. The art treasures of Petworth were then shown to conducted parties at 11am, 12 noon, 2pm and 3pm, Tuesdays and Thursdays, with the park open to the general public. Petworth became a property of the National Trust in 1947.

PETWORTH (2)
West Sussex

Petworth House.

The previous card shows how closely the town adjoins the back of Petworth House and in looking at this early view we see how Petworth church spire almost seems to emerge from the roof of the house. A photograph from the same vantage point today gives an aesthetically more acceptable view of the west front: what Pevsner described as 'Sir Charles Barry's monstrous spindly spire' was dismantled in 1947, having been added to the church's south-east tower in 1827.

It may equally be felt that this long frontage is somewhat featureless, and when the house was built at the end of the seventeenth century there was a central dome to break the outline, but this was removed soon after building was completed. Also lost are many of the trees appearing in this scene, not just by natural wastage but as a result of the severe storms which have swept the county in recent years, devastating much of Capability Brown's original planting.

This card was published by John Evelyn Wrench who, early in the century, pioneered the sale of postcards in museums, art galleries and other places open to the public, reproducing the exhibits on display.

BADDESLEY CLINTON
Warwickshire

This delightful medieval moated manor house stands within a few miles of Birmingham's depressing high-rise tower blocks but is mercifully concealed from any sight of them. Successive owners have managed to conserve much of value and interest, both structurally and as regards contents. This view faces the Great Hall with its stained-glass windows, now set in brick, and original timberwork still appearing in the gables.

The postcard is of interest, however, in that it prominently depicts a service wing, right, which was added towards the end of the nineteenth century, not many years before the card was published. It shows that mock timber-framing and even concrete blocks can be successfully blended to preserve harmony and dignity.

While most of the ivy and other growth has been cleared, the courtyard otherwise remains much as shown on old pictures, with the Ferrers arms as a floral feature set in the lawn in correct heraldic colours. The original completeness of many rooms shown adds to the atmosphere of Baddesley Clinton which also offers a priest hole, an indelible blood stain, and a ghost-haunted library with a tale alleging murder most foul!

SHUGBOROUGH HALL
Staffordshire

Shugborough Hall, Great Haywood.

Since a television programme in 1974, a strange mystery has kept surfacing in the notable grounds of this historic house. Among the garden monuments is the enigmatic Shepherds' Monument containing a carved copy of a painting by Nicholas Poussin, *Et in Arcadia Ego*, and carrying the strange inscription *OUOSVAVV*. It has been suggested that Poussin's painting is part of a complex code incorporated within a carving in the church of the little French village of Rennes-le Château, and associated with the lost treasure of the Knights Templars.

More prosaically, this scene of the west front records appearances prior to changes, both to the layout of the formal garden and structural alterations made in the 1920s, when first-floor windows and elevations were remodelled and the house was faced with stucco.

WOOLSTHORPE MANOR
Lincolnshire

A postcard reproduction of an old print sent by visitors in 1908 who wrote: 'The house is much nicer looking than the picture in reality'. Basically this is a small seventeenth-century farmhouse which owes its tourist interest to associations with Sir Isaac Newton. Born here on Christmas Day 1642, he returned during the plague years of 1665-6 to formulate some of his great scientific and mathematical discoveries, including the law of gravitation, supposedly after watching apples falling off the trees in the orchard.

THE GREYFRIARS
Worcester

ANCIENT FRIARY, FRIAR STREET, WORCESTER

One of the Trust's most handsome town properties is this former guest house for a Franciscan friary in the centre of the city. It is of late fifteenth-century construction with subsequent additions followed by conversion to shops, as shown here. It has now been fully restored with panelled rooms furnished and an attractive garden established.

Perhaps inevitably, the shop nearest the camera in this view had become 'Ye Olde Curiositie Shoppe', while William McHarg, next door, was a hairdresser who, as was often the case with barbers, also repaired umbrellas. A hanging umbrella sign can just be discerned above the man watching the photographer. Greyfriars is open only at certain times and visitors should consult the National Trust Handbook.

SUDBURY HALL
Derbyshire

This former seat of the Lords Vernon is in the heart of the Meynell Hunt country and many such scenes as this have taken place in front of the fine seventeenth-century mansion. Hugo Meynell (1717-1800) is acknowledged as the 'father of modern fox hunting' and was Master of the Quorndon from 1753 until his death. He also hunted from Hoar Cross Hall, his family seat in Staffordshire.

The Lord Vernon of the early nineteenth century established a notable pack of hounds to rival those of his 'commoner' neighbour, dressing his hunt staff in bright orange with low hats as opposed to Mr Meynell's scarlet with high hats. The Hoar Cross Hunt was later to become the Meynell Hunt and when, in 1873-4, new kennels were built (still in use), they were situated near to Sudbury Hall as this was a more central position for the Meynell country.

The scene on the postcard can be dated to *c.*1903. The road past Sudbury Hall subsequently became a very busy thoroughfare but a by-pass has now restored tranquillity to the estate village of Sudbury adjoining the hall and the Vernon Arms.

SUDBURY HALL
Lord Vernon's Coming of Age, 1909

The close ties that usually existed between 'big house' and tenantry was well demonstrated when there was a coming of age celebration. At Sudbury the 8th baron, who had been a page at Edward VII's Coronation, succeeded to the title when he was ten, so that this occasion also marked his taking over of the Vernon estates. On Thursday 30 September 1909, on the family's Poynton estate in Cheshire, tenants, village children and miners from Poynton collieries were 'sumptuously entertained'.

The next day the scene switched to Sudbury for a repeat performance. The village was decorated throughout and the customary triumphal arch erected. Over six hundred tenants were entertained on the park and the press elicited that the caterer, Mr. Ramsden of Derby, would eventually have served over ten thousand people in connection with this event. The tenants presented a grandfather clock, cigar case and match box, £65 having been raised. Old English sports followed along with variety turns, dancing, a children's tea and firework displays, with several bands in attendance. Those present at a champagne lunch received a crested fruit plate and a box containing cigars, cigarettes and matches.

A local photographer recorded the occasion for postcards which no doubt sold well as an inexpensive memento of a grand day out.

KEDLESTON HALL
Derbyshire

K edleston has a long record of opening to visitors. In the 1860s it could be seen daily 'from 11 o'clock a.m. till 3 pm'. There was then a period when it ceased to open at all.

'It used to be open to the public weekly, but now, unfortunately it is never' lamented the author of *Pleasant Rambles Round Derby* in 1894. In describing the mansion it is surprising how, having invariably quoted Dr Johnson's satirical comment on its potential as a town hall, nineteenth-century guide books pass on to the natural spring within the grounds as being a greater wonder than the work of Robert Adam. Thus, Dugdale in the 1840s:

'Taken inwardly it operates as a diuretic and affords relief in cases of the gravel. It has also been found efficacious, from external application, in cutaneous diseases, ulcerous complaints &c. In the summer it is frequently used by the inhabitants of Derby as a substitute for malt liquor; the charge of carriage, which is one penny per quart, affords subsistence for a few poor people of the neighbourhood.'

This postcard shows the Music Room in Edwardian days. Adam's gilded mahogany organ and most of the pictures remain unaltered but some changes to the furniture and removal of drapes and a miscellany of small items has substituted today's elegance for this more 'lived-in' appearance.

TATTERSHALL CASTLE
Lincolnshire

Tattershall Castle. Fireplace on First Floor.
No. 653. Copyright. Carlton

This property was dramatically rescued by Lord Curzon of Kedleston. The chief feature of the enormous rooms in the tower-keep is the rich series of fine stone fireplaces. Represented on the carved panels is a purse with drawstrings, emblem of the Treasurer of England, and incorporated in the design by a holder of that office, Ralph, Lord Cromwell, when he built Tattershall *c*.1440.

In 1911 these fireplaces had been removed from their surrounds and were already crated in London for despatch to America. Lord Curzon purchased the castle and retrieved the fireplaces for return to their original settings - an event recently commemorated at the 75th anniversary of the opening of Tattershall to the public in 1914.

Lord Curzon described Tattershall as 'the most splendid piece of brickwork in England'. The near loss of its fireplaces prompted new legislation to protect historic monuments. At this time the 100-foot tower had been struck by lightning and was nearly derelict, while farm animals occupied the ground floor and the whole site had been despoiled for building materials.

BODIAM CASTLE
East Sussex

Adelightful early Edwardian painting by Wilfred Ball of the Royal Society of Etchers and Engravers, recording the castle as it looked at that time. Today's visitors again owe a debt to Lord Curzon who purchased Bodiam in 1917 and instituted urgent major conservation work, removing trees from splits in the masonry and eliminating the ivy, weeds and bushes which had made it a picturesque but dilapidated and rapidly deteriorating ruin. The moat was drained for repairs to the foundations and the present surrounding parkland created.

Built in 1386-9, Bodiam is a rare example of a private citizen, Sir Edward Dalyngrigge, being granted authority to construct his own castle, and it now stands as an imposing example of medieval military architecture, incorporating a handsome fortified courtyard manor house within the walls.

MONTACUTE HOUSE
Somerset

Interior Montacute House.

The National Trust acquired its second major country house *via* the Society for the Protection of Ancient Buildings to which it was presented by a generous donor, Mr E.E. Cook, in 1931. Pre-war visitors paid one shilling [5p] but saw only empty rooms as the contents had all been dispersed; most of what is now on show is provided from bequests, loans or gifts, together with pictures on loan from the National Portrait Gallery.

The postcard, *c*.1903, is therefore a glimpse of how the Great Hall looked just before its hereditary owners, the Phelips, left - a relaxed informality below the ancestral portraits. The house was then let to tenants who included Lord Curzon, so Montacute is yet another present Trust property where he carried out some refurbishment. Although he was the owner of Kedleston, it was mellow Montacute which he proclaimed as 'the most beautiful house in England'.

This postcard also shows the decorated plasterwork frieze by an unknown local craftsman described as 'Riding the Skimmington' - a traditional burlesque procession designed to ridicule henpecked husbands. The etymology of the phrase is uncertain but the theme is found in Spain and Scandinavia as well as in other parts of Britain.

ST MICHAEL'S MOUNT
Cornwall

In the first century bc a Sicilian historian, Diodorus Siculus, wrote of the Carthaginians trading for tin from an island off Britain called Ictis. 'At ebb tide, the land between the mainland and this island is left dry...' a perfect description of to-day's causeway approach.

The translation of its Cornish name means 'the grey rock in the woods' - given meaning with traces of a submerged forest off the base of the rock. In the time of Edward the Confessor, a Benedictine monastery was established here under the rule of the abbey of Mont-Saint-Michel, the island's more spectacular French 'twin'. The monastery buildings were fortified after the Dissolution and subsequently converted into a residence.

Celia Fiennes wrote in 1698: '...at the top is a pretty good house where the Governour lives sometymes ... there is a chaire or throne on the top from whence they can discover a great way at sea and here they put up lights to direct shipps.'

The postcard is a good quality reproduction by the firm of the noted photographer, Frith of Reigate, of the engraving by S. and N. Buck, dated 1731. Samuel Buck (1696-1779) was a topographical draughtsman and engraver who has left us 428 views of abbeys and castles, 4 of country seats and 83 general views of towns, an invaluable pictorial record. This one belongs to a period when he was assisted by his brother Nathaniel. They spent their summers drawing and travelling and the winters engraving and printing.

THE CHEVY CHASE ROOM - ST. MICHAEL'S MOUNT
Cornwall

St. Michael's Mount Castle, Chevy Chase Room.

So-called from the plaster hunting frieze added in the seventeenth century to what was once the refectory and later the Great Hall, with its fifteenth century timbered roof. No less a personage than Queen Victoria herself has left us an account of her visit here on the royal yacht in 1846 with Prince Albert and five-years-old 'Bertie' (Edward VII):

'The dining room, made out of the refectory, is very pretty. It is surrounded by a frieze representing ancient hunting.' Chevy Chase has its origins in events surrounding the rivalry between the Percy family of Northumberland and the Douglas family of Scotland.

The Queen's guide, as was usually the case when even distinguished visitors called at a house in the owner's absence, was 'the old housekeeper - a nice tidy old woman' although the Queen had earlier commented that the Cornish were 'a very noisy, talkative race, and speak a kind of English hardly to be understood'. The party then left what the journal describes as a 'nice house to live in, as there are so many good rooms in it .... the view from the top is very beautiful and very extensive.' As they departed, Albert made a 'beautiful little sketch' of the scene that today's visitors record with their cameras.

KNOLE
Kent

CALKE ABBEY.

KNOLE
Kent

There is no National Trust property having a finer early picture postcard record than Knole. With the full encouragement of Lady Sackville-West, the Sevenoaks publishing firm of Salmon, still producing postcards today, commissioned a local watercolour artist, C. Essenhigh Corke, to produce a series of coloured *facsim* views - the name given to facsimile postcard reproductions of oil or watercolour paintings, which many people framed as being miniature works of art in their own right. In 1904-5 he covered most of the principal rooms at Knole as well as painting a number of outdoor scenes. Some of his later paintings used for cards are dated 1912-13. W.C. Addison and A. Harding Norwood are two other postcard artists who also worked at Knole.

The cards illustrated here are from C. Essenhigh Corke's first sets and show the King James I bedroom and a scene in the grounds. The latter, posted locally by Annie to Alice, carries a message which exemplifies the great enthusiasm at this time for collecting.

Annie writes: 'How is the P.C. collection progressing? I now have over 200 and you see that I have reserved the peacock for you.'

As well as this pictorial record Knole has featured prominently in literature. Vita Sackville-West, creator of the Trust garden at Sissinghurst, wrote *Knole and the Sackvilles* as well as making Knole the inspiration for Chevron in *The Edwardians*. Her friend, Virginia Woolf, based her novel *Orlando* largely on the house and family of Knole.

This great mansion, with its magnificent contents, is arranged around seven courtyards, reputedly with fifty-two staircases and three hundred and sixty-five rooms. "This at least is the legend," writes V. Sackville-West, "I do not know that anyone has ever troubled to verify it."

CRAGSIDE
Northumberland

Drawing Room, Cragside, Rothbury

T he massive marble and alabaster chimney-piece by W.R. Lethaby dominates the Drawing Room at Cragside, seen here within twenty years of its completion in 1883-4 to the designs of the architect Richard Norman Shaw. He had created Cragside for Sir William, later Lord, Armstrong, from a small lodge.

Among its claims to fame is that it was the first big country house to be lit by electricity as well as being the first house to utilise hydro-electric power. Cragside contained many other technical innovations including the use of hydraulics, Sir William being the first industrialist to apply hydraulic to cranes. The difficulties of the site, however, created a few problems and the Drawing Room is a considerable distance from the other principal rooms. It was lit from above, apart from one recessed bay window, and was also planned for picture display. Most of the paintings seen here were sold soon after this photograph was taken.

CILGERRAN CASTLE
Dyfed

Cilgerran Castle, Pembrokeshire.

Among popular Edwardian postcards were *Moonlight Series* which sought to give an unusual or romantic look to a familiar scene. Many of these cards were, in fact, faked from daytime scenes, sometimes with quite comical effects, such as impossible shadows or the presence of ladies holding up sunshades. 'Sad perversions of taste' complained the *Picture Postcard Magazine* in 1901.

Long before the National Trust acquired the thirteenth-century ruins in 1938, they had become a tourist attraction. Eighteenth- and nineteenth-century visitors often made their approach by boat rather than by road, coming up the Teifi River from Cardigan. The ubiquitous Turner was among artists who portrayed the dramatic outlines of the castle high on the rocky promontory above the river gorge.

From an earlier castle on the site the fascinating Princess Nesta was reputedly 'abducted' by a son of the Prince of Powys who became another of her lovers, and Cilgerran's association with her added to the castle's romantic appeal. It is now in the guardianship of Cadw: Welsh Historic Monuments.

SELWORTHY
Somerset

Early coloured postcards vary from the inferior and blurred to magnificent examples faithfully reproducing works of art in miniature. Until 1907 postcard colouring was done by hand using various lithographic processes from a three-colour system devised in Germany by Joseph Albert, to scenes which might involve applying teens of colours, each one requiring a different block. In 1907 the *autochrome* process introduced photographic coloured printing and this 'Colour Photo' view of Selworthy Green is an early example. It suggests a carefully posed group of locals and visitors.

'This place', says the sender, 'is sweetly pretty on the side of a hill overlooking the valley with Dunkery Beacon in the distance.' He then qualifies enthusiasm for scenery by commenting, 'I hope we may be able to get back on Friday. Rather tired of nothing to do.'

The National Trust owns more than 12,000 acres of Exmoor, over half of it ensuring preservation of its original moorland character. The area embraces Dunkery and Selworthy beacons and a group of small farms and villages including Selworthy.

CHIDDINGSTONE
Kent

B ritish picture postcard views date from 1894 as mentioned in the Introduction. They were court size cards, approximately 4½ x 3½ inches, the largest size then permitted by the Post Office. Since space had to be left for a message (only the address could be written on the back) the pictures were usually quite small and it was only from 1 November, 1899, that the larger size card, 5½ x 3½ inches, was authorised.

Here, however, we have a later version which falls between the two sizes and this is because it is an advertising card specially designed to fit the container in which it was given away with brands of cigarettes manufactured by Godfrey Phillips Ltd., and associated companies. Various series included 'Beauty Spots of the Homeland' and No.12 in a set of 30 is this card of Chiddingstone where the National Trust owns the Castle Inn and the splendid row of sixteenth- and seventeenth-century houses, reproduced here from an original painting. The houses are not open to visitors.

MOSELEY OLD HALL
Staffordshire

Old Moseley Hall,
near Wolverhampton.
Charles II. hid here after the Battle
of Worcester, 1651.

This postcard, with its inset of Charles II, is something of a curiosity. Visitors to Moseley Old Hall can perhaps be forgiven if their initial impression is one of disappointment. From the outside the first sighting suggests, except for the chimneys, a nineteenth-century house. The hall actually dates back to *c.* 1600 and might well not have survived without a considerable restoration about 1870 when the outer walls were covered in brick and the Elizabethan windows replaced by casements. Only inside does one find the original timber framework and panelling and there is much of interest to see, the house figuring notably in the epic of the restoration of the monarchy.

Although this sketch may satisfy ideas of how the house ought to have looked, it certainly never did look like this. At first one wonders if the artist was using considerable licence to portray the house he perhaps expected to see. A. Chatwin in *Staffordshire History* (Volume 2, 1985) reveals that the original titled sketch by J.Fullwood in *Etchings of Old Wolverhampton* (1882) is of Northycote Farm, half a mile from Moseley Old Hall. Quite simply Mr Fullwood seems to have drawn the wrong house and the error is perpetuated on the postcard.

KINVER EDGE
Staffordshire

Forest Rock House Museum, Kinver.

The Trust owns nearly 300 acres of this high heath and woodland, the remains of a royal hunting forest and, earlier, an Iron Age settlement. Legends associate the site with pagan giants and pre-Reformation hermits, but most fascinating were the rock dwellings cut into the soft sandstone that provided homes occupied over many centuries.

In the early twentieth century tenants were recorded as paying an average of about £8 a year rent to the lord of the manor. Some houses were lived in until the 1960s but their present state hardly gives an idea of the extent to which the caverns were 'improved' by means of casement windows, bricked door frames and even tiled gables. Smoke from house fires could be seen curling out from the hillside.

This card from the mid-1920s shows exploitation of the site at Astle's Rock for a museum displaying a curious collection of miscellaneous objects. The owner, Mr. Fairbrother, also opened a tea garden, while the Fletcher family, who lived at Holy Austin Rock, were featured on many popular postcards purchased by visitors who once flocked here in great numbers for a summer outing.

POLDHU
Cornwall

A mile from Mullion village at Poldhu, the Italian inventor Guglielmo Marconi erected his first high-power wireless transmitting station. On 12 December 1901, Marconi was in Newfoundland where an aerial was raised by means of launching a kite and on this primitive receiving apparatus, faint crackling morse signals were picked up from Poldhu, the first-ever transatlantic wireless message. In 1924 Marconi's revolutionary short wave beam system was successfully pioneered from here.

To quote the National Trust Guide: 'Seventy years ago most of the fifty-five acres [now] owned by the Trust was covered in lattice masts, cables, guy ropes, aerials and sheds, all now vanished.'

Mary's card to Bessie 'for your collection' was posted in 1905 and captures the lost scene on this historic headland. The Marconi memorial put up by the company stands today within an area of extensive Trust ownership of magnificent coastal scenery.

ROBIN HOOD'S BAY
North Yorkshire

AEROPLANE VIEW OF COAST LINE AT ROBIN HOODS BAY. (3256)

A few aerial photographs were taken in the nineteenth century from balloons. Activity by aeroplanes increased rapidly from around the year 1909, when Bleriot flew the Channel. The country's first aviation meetings were being held at places such as Doncaster, Blackpool, Bournemouth and Burton-on-Trent, where local aerial views were produced as postcards. It was after the First World War, however, that aerial photographs became popular. F.L.Willis and Claude Graham White established Aerofilms in 1919, and this firm now has archives of half a million pictures, many appearing as postcards. Other aerial photographers included Surrey Flying Services of Croydon.

Here we have a *Photochrom* card showing an aeroplane view 'by arrangement with the Aircraft Manufacturing Co. Ltd.' It is a scene taken which brings to life lines in the current National Trust Handbook: 'Here the Trust's ownership [of cliffland] is greatest with the whole of the headland north of Robin Hood's Bay, Boggle Hole, the curiously incised inlet in the middle of the Bay and most of the southern end and headland ...'

The very first property to come to the National Trust was a gift of 4½ acres of coastal land, Dinas Oleu above Barmouth. Today the Trust owns over 500 miles of coastline.

DOVEDALE
Derbyshire

The Stepping Stones, Dovedale, Ashbourne. North Stafford Railway.

Dovedale is a region which has long been popular with visitors even though, well into this century, tourists were solemnly warned that 'by far the greater part can only be traversed by the pedestrian ... fallen stones under foot and the rough stone walls every few hundred yards will make his progress very slow.' It did not deter large numbers from flocking in - especially by train - and it was a favourite spot for Sunday School and other outings.

This view is an example of railway publicity, most of the old companies issuing post-cards of attractive places on their routes - often the same pictures once featured inside railway carriages. The North Staffordshire Railway approached Dovedale at Ashbourne and the London & North Western Railway's line continued up to Buxton, with stations serving nearby points such as Thorpe Cloud and Alsop-en-le-Dale. Today it is estimated that over half a million people a year come to Dovedale, causing serious problems of wear and tear and the need for footpath conservation.

The card shows the donkeys once available for public hire, but perhaps the most dramatic entry to Dovedale was by Dean Langton of Clogher in 1761. He attempted to ride a horse up the slope near Reynard's Cave with a daring young lady, a Miss la Roche, seated behind him. The horse slipped and fell, killing the Dean. The young lady, badly injured, was saved by her hair catching in a thorn bush.

VISITORS TO DOVEDALE, 1912

Chamber of Trade.
Picnic to Dovedale. June 26/12.

A typical party of visitors enjoying a sunny summer afternoon in Dovedale. On 26 June 1912, some fifty members of the Burton-on-Trent Chamber of Trade left by the 1.40 pm train of the North Staffordshire Railway for their annual outing.

This was a Wednesday, half-day closing in the town, and the party included a local photographer who took his camera with him to combine business with pleasure. Everyone dressed very formally for the occasion and they probably did little more than take a gentle stroll at the easy end of the dale before assembling for their picnic in the grounds of the nearby Peveril of the Peak Hotel, seen in the background.

This postcard was carefully retained as a souvenir for 55 years before being sent to 'Lily' in 1967 with the message: 'I thought you might like to keep this. I think it is excellent of your parents and my brother-in-law.' Other identifications follow and cards with such information are a bonus for today's local and social history collectors.

THE WINNATS AND MAM TOR
Derbyshire

Entrance to the Winnats, Castleton.   "Scott" Series No. 81.

It is not easy to reconcile this postcard scene with today's busy route from Castleton to Chapel-en-le-Frith, although it used to be the main road Buxton coach. The closure of the road round Mam Tor because of landslips has now added to present-day traffic pressures while the building on the left is the entrance for the popular Speedwell Cavern which attracts more visitors' cars.

The name Winnats is a corruption of 'wind-gates' and we see it early this century still a gated track. Go on a day when the wind is howling down the limestone gorge and the aptness of the name will be all too apparent. The pass itself commences its winding journey below 400ft cliffs just beyond the cavern entrance where postcards like this were on sale. Mam Tor, the 'shivering mountain' is a geological freak with an Iron Age camp on its summit.

That intrepid traveller, Celia Fiennes, came here and warned that it was 'very dangerous to ascend', but it attracts many visitors on foot who enjoy its wide and impressive view points.

BOX HILL
Surrey

The Look-out, Box Hill, Dorking.

HISTORY OF BOXHILL.

Boxhill, the summit of which is 600 feet above sea level, is undoubtedly the best known and the most popular hill on the North Downs. It takes its name, of course, from the box trees which are said to have been planted during the thirteenth century.

It is to the generosity of the late Leopold Salomons Esq, of Norbury Park, Mickleham, that the public owe the privilege of using the hill as a pleasure resort. Mr. Salomons, to save the land from the hands of the builders, bought the property from Lord F. H. Pelham-Clinton Hope and presented it to the nation.

The views from the summit are very extensive, and looking South, the South Downs may be seen in the distance, whilst Reigate, Brockham, Leigh, and Newdigate are plainly visible. The River Mole, running through Betchworth Park, can easily be traced as far as Dorking, and looking south-west, Leith Hill Tower is a prominent landmark.

O ver the years publishers produced postcards for tourists designed to combine some basic information with the souvenir picture. Some, like this of Box Hill, are factual; others, like those of Avebury and White Horse Hill which follow, delve into the legendary past.

The National Trust owns or has covenants over a considerable acreage of Box Hill, now a designated country park. Mr Salomon's gift of the first 230 acres came to the Trust in 1914. Leith Hill with its tower, which can be seen from here, is the highest point in south-east England and both vantage points provide panoramic views.

AVEBURY
Wiltshire

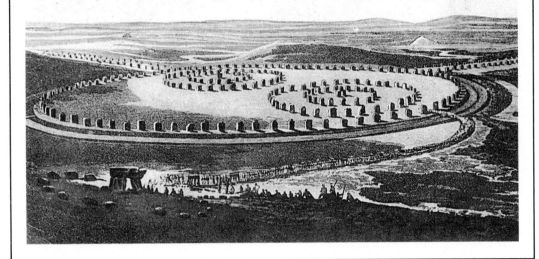

The Temple, Avebury. (A Restoration after J. Britton).

The Great Stone Circle, it is said, was approached by two avenues of 200 stones each, which took a sinuous course south-east and south-west, and represented a snake transmitted through a circle.

Stukeley puts its foundation at 1859 B.C., the year of the death of Sarah, Abraham's wife. It has been said by lord Avebury „The pretty little village of Avebury, like some beautiful parasite, has grown up at the expense and in the midst of the ancient temple."

Avebury is so extensive that it is difficult to appreciate it fully without lengthy exploration. The complete site (henge) covers 27 acres and the overall layout is made more difficult to follow by the presence of Avebury village within its bounds. The original purpose of this Megalithic ceremonial monument dating back to around 1800 b.c. is still uncertain. While much remains, it is tragic that so much more survived until comparatively recently. Seventeenth- and eighteenth-century destruction of standing stones was truly described by William Stukeley as 'barbarous massacre'.

The Sanctuary, another stone circle at the end of the remarkable Kennet Avenue, was not lost until the nineteenth century. This imaginative reconstruction attempts to reinstate the complete pattern of the circles and appeared as an illustration in the 1840s.

While still abounding with remains of antiquity, today's scene is a far cry from that described in the accompanying text which stresses the solitude of the district and says: 'You may just espy a solitary bare-footed shepherd boy watching his flocks nibbling the short thymy grass.' The site is in the care of English Heritage.

UFFINGTON CASTLE AND WHITE HORSE HILL
Oxfordshire

WHITE HORSE HILL, UFFINGTON.—"White Horse Hill," and then what a hill is White Horse Hill; there it stands, right above all the rest, nine hundred feet above the sea, and the boldest, bravest shape for a chalk hill that you ever saw. Let us go to the top of him and see what is to be found there. Ay, you may well wonder and think it odd you never heard this before. Yes, it's a magnificent Roman Camp and no mistake, with gates and ditch and mounds all as complete as it was twenty years after the old rogue left it, on the highest point of which they say you can see eleven counties. White Horse Hill, Uffington, may be seen on the G.W.R. Down Side between Uffington and Shrivenham. See Tom Brown's School Days.

In 1822 Thomas Hughes was baptised in Uffington church where there is now a commemorative plaque. The postcard quotes from his classic book *Tom Brown's School Days* (1857). The passage probably conveys the atmosphere of this fascinating site rather than strict historical accuracy because there are still debatable theories on aspects of both castle and horse.

The eight-acre hill-fort is of the Iron Age; the White Horse may date from the same period, although some archaeologists advocate a later date to make it Anglo-Saxon. While there is considerable evidence of horse worship in the Iron Age, it may have been a later tribal emblem, but it is certainly one of our oldest chalk-cut hill figures, 350 ft long and 130 ft high.

Fanciful legend has brought St George here as well so that below the horse we have Dragon Hill. English Heritage have the guardianship of these sites.

PARADISE
Derbyshire/Staffordshire

Entrance to Paradise, Ilam.

This 1903 photograph shows a scene equally idyllic today and little altered from when two distinguished visitors explored it over two hundred years ago. Here the rivers Manifold and Hamps, after their mysterious journeys underground, reappear and join together to flow into the Dove.

When Johnson and Boswell saw them in 1777, Johnson was only convinced of the phenomenon when, as Boswell subsequently wrote, they 'had the attestation of the gardener [at Ilam Hall] who said he had put in corks where the Manifold sinks into the ground and had caught them in a net placed before one of the openings where the water bursts out.'

Paradise Walk, while taking one a little away from the river, provides a superb woodland panorama, perhaps at its most spectacular when dressed in autumn colours.

VISITORS TO HAYBURN WYKE
North Yorkshire

A poster, just discernible under the awning, referring to the Hayburn Wyke Private Estate, was the key to identifying this busy scene, probably photographed in the early 1920s. A rambling club or similar party are enjoying afternoon tea at the Hayburn Wyke Hotel which still remains in business today.

Present Trust land adjoins the hotel and incorporates its former pleasure grounds. From Victorian times this was a favourite resort for tourists who could travel via the now defunct Scarborough to Whitby railway line and visit the woodlands and the cliffs above the small rocky inlet. Publicity posters proclaimed: 'Romantic Bay and Scenery - Hotel in Beautiful Grounds.'

The area is now within the North York Moors National Park and includes a nature reserve. It is crossed by the Cleveland Way long-distance footpath.

CLENT HILLS
Hereford & Worcester

FOUR STONES, SUMMIT OF CLENT HILLS.

The many Edwardian visitors who climbed to the summit of the Clent Hills, nearly 1,000 feet high, and sent off souvenir postcards like this one, no doubt helped to perpetuate the claim for 'The Stonehenge of the Midlands' but the Four Stones were actually erected as a feature in the mid-eighteenth century. There are fine views and many places of interest to be found all around this popular walking area, long a favourite resort for residents of Birmingham and the Black Country, and indeed for walkers from much further afield.

For 30 September 1934, the Manchester group of the 'Out-o'-doors' Fellowship made the following arrangements: To Birmingham for Clent Hills - total fares about 5/8d (around 28p). Train from Manchester London Road (LMS) 9.45 am, due Birmingham New Street, 12.15 pm Return 8.10 pm, due back 10.30 pm Leader, Mr F.W. Clenton.

This was a period of great enthusiasm for cycling and walking. Thomas Cook & Son Ltd. were offering 8-day walking tours of the 'Romantic Rhineland' for six guineas (£6.30) covering travel from London, full-board accommodation for five nights, gratuities and services of a leader throughout.

MOUNT GRACE PRIORY
North Yorkshire

Mount Grace Priory.   Yorkshire.

J. R. R. E.

'Visited by train and shanks' pony, June 1911' says the faded inscription just discernible on the back of the souvenir card.

Railway timetables of the period advertised many special rate day or weekend tours for ramblers or cyclists, often planned to allow the traveller to disembark at one station and pick up an evening train at another some distance away. Reaching Mount Grace our visitors would have found the typical "ivy-covered romantic ruins" much appreciated at this time.

This was a Carthusian monastery founded in 1397. The order was one of strict seclusion, the monks living in separate cells the design of which can still be recognised. Each cell had piped water, a gardrobe and a hatch with a right-angled bend through which food was handed, unseen, to the contemplative monk living in complete isolation.

The site today is in the care of English Heritage, having come to the Trust in 1953.

LETOCETUM (WALL)
Staffordshire

A 1902 guidebook reports that 'scarcely any foundations are visible' on this Roman site though 'many items have been dug up'. There was some excavation during the nineteenth century and in the period 1912-14. The Trust acquired the site in 1924 and by the 1930s, Arthur Mee in *The King's England* could enthuse about 'an imperial city... scheduled as an ancient monument'.

Wall, in fact, was a small Romano-British town serving as a posting station for the nearby Watling Street. An interesting museum and extended excavations are now open but the principal feature is the town bath-house, the best example of its type in the country.

The postcard is one of a series made while excavations were in progress, revealing the hypocaust by which the bath-house was heated. This site is in the guardianship of English Heritage.

HOUSESTEADS
Northumberland

PRETORIUM HOUSESTEADS. 27.

Housesteads, or, to give it the Roman name, Vercovicium, provides the finest British example of a well-defined layout of a complete Roman fort. This rather untidy postcard scene, however, seems fully to justify H.V. Morton who wrote, as late as 1927, in *In Search Of England*: 'The Roman wall across England is the most marvellous engineering enterprise in the country, and it is time the Office of Works took charge of it and made it a guarded ancient monument.'

Three years later Housesteads and some splendid sections of the wall nearby were given to the National Trust which later built the adjoining museum to display the many antiquities found on the site and to illustrate its fascinating story.

LAVENHAM GUILDHALL
Suffolk

One of the delightful timber-framed buildings that grace Lavenham, this was the sixteenth-century hall of the Guild of Corpus Christi. After a checkered history as prison, workhouse, almshouse, nursery school and even a 'British Restaurant' it now houses an exhibition of local history and of the wool trade which once gave Lavenham its importance. It is hardly surprising that the interior suffered considerably, now retaining little of its original panelling or carving.

A local photographer recorded this bare interior scene with old moulded beams and joists, contrasting with some rather bizarre gaslight fittings and a great fireplace occupied by a coke stove

BOARSTALL TOWER
Buckinghamshire

Boarstall Tower

Those who seek for romantic, tragic or dramatic stories about an ancient edifice will find them in plenty in old histories of Boarstall Tower. The tradition is that one Nigel, a huntsman, was given land by Edward the Confessor after slaying a vicious boar which was terrorising the king's hunting ground in Bernwood Forest.

In 1312 the Lord of Boarstall obtained licence to fortify the mansion that had been built here. The present tower, though altered in the sixteenth and seventeenth centuries, formed the great gatehouse.

Boarstall was the centre of much civil war activity before again becoming a peaceful 'noble seat'. It passed by marriage in the late seventeenth century to Sir John Aubrey. In 1777, the six-year-old heir of Boarstall, son of another Sir John, tragically died. His nurse prepared a gruel for him using oatmeal with which poison had been mixed to kill rats. The nurse became demented, the mother died of shock and grief, and Sir John promptly ordered the demolition of the mansion, only this tower being allowed to remain.
[Visiting only by written appointment]

CARTMEL PRIORY GATEHOUSE
Cumbria

This postcard reflects changes in the townscape as well as in the property now owned by the Trust.

The Augustinian priory at Cartmel was founded in 1188 by William Mareschall, Earl of Pembroke. The gatehouse dates from *c.*1330 and is all that remains of the priory except for the splendid medieval church, restored after the Dissolution to serve the parish. The gatehouse, in many ways resembling the fortified defensive border towers which are a feature of the north country, survived to be used as a court-house and as a grammar school. Turret and battlements were removed and other windows added, but by the time of the postcard it was in poor condition.

A slightly earlier photograph shows the shop on the left to have been the unlikely combination of seedsman and draper with an advertising board outside for McDougall's Sheep Dip. *The Cavendish Arms* is prominently indicated 'through the passage'. The building was rescued by a local historian, repaired and given to the Trust in 1946.

PAXTON'S TOWER
Dyfed

Paxton Tower, near Llandilo.

The Trust has its share of follies and this not unattractive triangular tower commands a wide view over the lush valley of the River Towy. Built in 1811 by Sir William Paxton as a Nelson memorial, it exemplifies the romantic taste of its period, a striking architectural feature superimposed upon a pastoral landscape. The postcard, obviously long retained as a souvenir, says: 'We climbed up here on July 22nd., 1904.'

CHIRK CASTLE
Clwyd

Chirk Castle is one of the Marcher fortresses, dating from 1310, which became a residence with state rooms showing decorative styles from the sixteenth to the nineteenth centuries. In 1985 former staff employed at Chirk before the Second World War met for a reunion and recorded reminiscences of life in the servants' hall in the days when this, like many other Trust properties, was still a private house.

Often up at 5 am, former maids told how they wore velvet carpet slippers as they moved around so as not to disturb guests. One lady, a kitchen maid from 1935 to 1941, recalled that she earned £5 a month but maintained that despite the hard work 'it was a good life'. Some servants married from within the house although male and female quarters were strictly out of bounds to each other.

The servants' hall displays stern messages from an earlier period: 'No noise, no strife, nor swear at all; But all be decent in the hall' as well as 'Rules To Be Observed Here'. The kitchen area, with some portraits of past servants, is one of many interesting rooms open at Chirk.

The Edwardian postcard shows Adam's Tower, a name of unknown derivation but the part of the castle which best retains the character of the early fourteenth century.

PENRHYN CASTLE
Gwynedd

PENRHYN CASTLE, BANGOR.

A great construction costing nearly £½ million in the period 1827-40 has given us this remarkable example of neo-Norman architecture - although Hutchinson's *Beautiful Britain* called it 'a style which the critical may not desire to see repeated'.

Keeps such as Rochester and Hedingham were the inspiration for the massive tower commanding extensive views over the area and the largest estate owned by the Trust. Today the furnished castle also contains an industrial museum and other displays and exhibitions. The site was a palace of the kings of North Wales as long ago as the eighth century. Associated with the lost Elizabethan house is the 'Hirlas Horn' from which servants drank on special occasions, emptying the contents at one go and then blowing the horn to signify that their work was well done.

Queen Victoria and Prince Albert were early visitors to the 'new' mansion, and King Edward VII and Queen Alexandra stayed here in 1894, as Prince and Princess of Wales, when Edward became the first Prince of Wales to attend an Eisteddfod.

FOUNTAINS ABBEY AND STUDLEY ROYAL
North Yorkshire

FOUNTAINS ABBEY.

O f many postcards issued, the largest monastic ruins in Britain and the notable landscaped gardens of Studley Royal, 1720-40, are represented here by one published early in the twentieth century for 'The Proprietors of Colman's Starch'.

Advertising cards, in fact, often made up quite a proportion of those found in old collections. Given away free to help promote various products or publications, many were of quite pleasing design as in this series. This was a product most housewives would then be using on washday. Many firms, whose enamelled advertisements also covered railway stations of the period, made use of the picture postcard in this way, depicting a wide range of subjects.

Fountains takes its name from springs found near the first simple shelter set up in 1132 by a group of monks from the Benedictine Abbey of York, who broke away to establish a house of the more austere Cistercian order.

The gardens of Studley Royal combine naturalism and formalism in a landscape of water gardens, woodlands and the valley of the River Skell, leading up to the magnificent abbey ruins. The park, gardens and abbey were acquired in 1983 and soon headed the list for Trust attendance figures, reaching 300,000 visitors during 1990.

STUDLEY ROYAL

Studley Royal, near Ripon

The postcard records a feature that can no longer be seen - the house which was burnt in 1945 and subsequently demolished. Postcards form a valuable pictorial library of lost houses and there are instances where they are the only surviving record. At Studley the stables were converted into a new house (not open to the public).

Fire, scourge of so many mansions, here destroyed a house described in 1840 as 'an elegant seat ... handsome and commodious ...' with 'pleasure grounds particularly worthy of attention.' In 1864 'the domain of Studley opens up to the public every day except Sunday until five o'clock in the evening.'

The National Trust itself has not escaped the fire hazard. The fine seventeenth-century house at Coleshill in Berkshire was destroyed in 1952 shortly before the estate came to the Trust. Dunsland House in Devon was newly repaired and refurnished with substantial aid from the Historic Buildings Council, when fire completely destroyed it in 1967. Only a memorial tablet now marks the site.

Nostell Priory suffered a serious fire in 1980 and most recently, there was Uppark. In some cases the Trust has been able to utilise valuable items salvaged from fires. At Montacute, for example, there is now a marble chimney-piece from Coleshill in the Drawing-Room; needlework hangings can also be seen which survived the fire in 1927 at Stoke Edith in Herefordshire.

CASTLERIGG STONE CIRCLE
Cumbria

Keswick. The Druids Circle.

The postcard pre-dates Trust acquisition in 1913 but the scene remains unchanged. Recently this site became a subject of the debate between parties wanting to carry out archaeological excavation and the Trust advocating that the mystery and isolation of some sites justifies undisturbed conservation. In 1902 visitors via the Cockermouth, Keswick & Penrith Railway cheerfully accepted it as *The Druids Circle* or *The Druid Stones.*

Baddeley's noted guidebook had this quaint comment: 'They form, as Pat might say, an oval circle of about 35 yards diameter, and are of various shapes and sizes, the tallest being a fair 2 feet above your head. As to their numbers, count them if you can or will. The natives say you can't and the ordinary tourist says he won't. At any rate, as the old woman said of the Commandments, 'there's plenty on 'em'. An *extraordinary* tourist gives the number as 38, 13 of which form an oblong in the east quarter.'

Canon Rawnsley, one of the founders of the National Trust, was among those instrumental in acquiring the site, which is now under the guardianship of English Heritage.

BLAISE HAMLET
Avon

Blaise Hamlet, Henbury.

An unusual and distinctive Trust property, 4 miles from the centre of Bristol, is this delightful group of ten cottages around a green, each one different from its neighbour but combining to form a complete creation of the picturesque.

The architect of Blaise Hamlet was John Nash and it was built by the Squire of Blaise Castle, John Harford, in 1810-11 as homes for retired retainers from his estate. Was it to provide greater privacy or perhaps to deter neighbourly gossip that no front door was positioned where it was visible from any of the others?

The castle is now a social history museum for the city of Bristol, the Trust acquiring the "hamlet" in 1943. The cottages are not open but there is access to view them from the green.

ROMAN BATH
5 Strand Lane, London

THE ROMAN BATH IN STRAND LANE,
St. Clement Danes, London.

Stepped concrete erection apparently screening Roman retaining wall to prevent slipping of land from sloping bank of Thames

Roman brickwork crusted with deposit from spring

Roman Brickwork

Marble Casing taken from Earl of Essex's bath (A.D. 1588)

Modern Concrete about 9 inches thick hiding original Red Roman Tile paving

By kind permission of " The Sphere."

'There was an old Roman bath in those days at the bottom of one of the streets out of the Strand - it may be there still - in which I have had many a cold plunge ... I tumbled head foremost into it and then went for a walk to Hampstead.' So speaks David Copperfield in Dickens's novel.

The postcard carries another personal reminiscence on the back: ' We went to see this Saturday morning, almost the very oldest bit of London, nearly 2,000 years old and the only bath into which the original spring still runs; there is also the bit of Roman lead pipe left.'

The picture is reproduced from the magazine *The Sphere* and it was then described as probably dating from the earliest period of Roman occupation in this country.

Measuring 15½ ft long, 6½ ft wide, 5 ft deep, and 30 ft below the present level of the Strand, its water was believed to come from an ancient Holy Well nearby. The bath was restored in the seventeenth century but its origins are disputed by experts.

Occasionally open, the bath can be seen from the adjoining pathway. It is maintained for the Trust by Westminster City Council and remains as an intriguing relic ignored by many of London's visitors.

DUNHAM MASSEY MILL
Cheshire

Seen here overgrown and dilapidated, this was typical of the 'natural and romantic' appearance which was once favoured for abandoned buildings, with very little appreciation of how this hastened deterioration. Happily, this fine building of 1616 was rescued in time and has now been restored to working order by the National Trust.

THE GEORGE INN
Southwark, London

An old Hostelrie of the 17th Century.
Ye Olde "George Inn," Southwark,
(77, BOROUGH HIGH STREET).
Where good olde English fare is still served as in ye Coaching Days.
PROPRIETRESS--MISS MURRAY.

Southwark, to the south of London Bridge, was noted for the many inns that lined the High Street. Chaucer's pilgrims set out from the *Tabard*, a near neighbour of the *George*, and there were many others famed as posting and coaching inns with their galleried courtyards and long histories of hospitality. The *George* survives today as the only remaining galleried inn in London.

The writer H.V. Morton commented that it had 'at last been safely gathered into the ample bosom of the National Trust'. This was in 1937 when it was donated by the London & North Eastern Railway. Mercifully it then withstood the London Blitz.

In the sixteenth century the inn on this site was known as the *St George* but it was totally destroyed in 1676 by the Great Fire of Southwark, a serious conflagration but one little heard of, being overshadowed by the Great Fire of London of 1666. The Southwark fire began, according to an old record, 'at one Mr. Walsh's, an oilman, betwixt the *George* and the *Tabard*'. The *George* was rebuilt in 1677 on the old plan, 'having open wooden galleries leading to the chambers on each side of the inn yard'. In the late nineteenth century all but the main galleries were removed but the *George* long remained true to its ancient traditions.

In his book *In Search of London* H.V. Morton recalls sleeping, as late as 1930 'in a huge four-poster bed so high from the floor that a flight of three mahogany steps was provided to help one up. There was no bathroom and the chambermaid carried in a hip-bath which, in the morning, was filled with buckets of warm water. The bedside light was a candle ... There were no modern comforts, no bells, no telephones, no running water and only the most rudimentary sanitation, yet the atmosphere was full of kindness and geniality.' This was when Miss Murray was the proprietress - the lady named on the advertising postcard based on a sketch dated 1923.

The *George* is now open during licensing hours and serves coffee, bar snacks and meals.

ABERCONWY HOUSE
Gwynedd

Aberconwy Old Temperance Hotel, Conway
Coffee Room, built a. D. 1400

Thihis survivor of the old medieval houses of Conway has been extensively sketched and photographed over the years. When the family who spent a holiday at Conway in 1908 sent this postcard, they had 'just finished lunch here before going to catch the 2 o'clock train to Bettws'.

Although the streets appear pleasantly traffic-free, it can be seen that already a warning triangle has been affixed to the corner overhang. The house now contains the Conwy Exhibition telling the story of this ancient borough.

UPPARK
West Sussex

This postcard scene of Edwardian serenity was sent from Uppark itself: 'I am sending you a view of our house.' The hunt is assembling on the grass terraces running up in front of the mansion. Eighty years later the National Trust guidebook could say: 'The passage of time seems hardly to have touched this remote and lovely house and the eighteenth-century interior looks much as it did ... over two centuries ago.'

Tragically, that scourge of so many country houses, fire, was to strike on the afternoon of 30 August 1989. Ironically, the house was still encased in scaffolding following extensive renovation, with gale damage repairs and other restoration work almost completed. Some difficulties with the water supply on this hot summer afternoon was perhaps the final irony.

In the 1650s, Edward Forde had given London its first reliable water supply system and it was his engineering skill and technical abilities which allowed his descendants to build Uppark on top of a hill with no natural water supply immediately available.

CLAYDON HOUSE
Buckinghamshire

Claydon House,

Novelist 'Miss Read' in *Miss Clare Remembers* portrays an old Crimean war veteran. He says of Florence Nightingale: 'We fair worshipped her out there and I see her once not long ago ... at Claydon. There's a big house there that the Verneys own and Miss Nightingale stays there sometimes with her sister. She was sitting with her in the garden and I stood behind a tree and looked at her. I thought to myself "If ever a lady deserves a rest it's that one".'

Today's visitors see the bedroom used by Florence when she stayed at the house and it reflected national regard for her, early this century, that postcards of Claydon often carried the caption:'Home of Florence Nightingale'. Florence's sister, Frances Partenope, was the wife of Sir Harry Verney; she edited the family papers which tell the fascinating and often sad story of the Verney family.

The pride of Claydon is its notable west wing but this is the south front, which had undergone alteration in 1860. This lawn has seen many activities besides tennis, such as the Volunteers on parade and, not surprisingly, gatherings of nursing organisations.

RIEVAULX TERRACE
North Yorkshire

One of the finest examples of eighteenth-century landscaping, the grass terrace above the ruins of Rievaulx Abbey runs for half a mile in a gentle curve, 60-100 yards in width but so contrived that, leaving one classical temple, its companion is not in view at the other end. Between them, avenues cut through the trees, give changing views of the medieval ruins. This terrace matched another built above Duncombe Park and there may have been an ambitious plan to join the two which would have produced a scenic sweep nearly 3 miles in length. As it was, the cutting of Rievaulx Terrace gave work to some 800 unemployed men.

This postcard is a close-up view of part of the painted ceiling in the Ionic Temple which was conceived as a summer-house where meals could be served from a basement kitchen. The ceiling was the work of an Italian decorator, Giovanni Borgnis, who worked in the uncomfortable but time-honoured way, lying on his back on scaffolding. (Duncombe Park and Rievaulx Abbey are not National Trust properties.)

HOUGHTON MILL
Cambridgeshire

The postcard fraternity still remains very loyal to the old names of 'lost' counties and this fine building has been in Cambridgeshire only since reorganisation of county boundaries removed Huntingdonshire from the map.

The scene is mid-Edwardian when the mill was still in full use. This particular building dates from the mid-seventeenth to the nineteenth century and was once thatched. The site, however, on an artificial island in the River Ouse, is of ancient usage and there are documentary records of a pre-Conquest mill on or near the site as well as accounts of its later history. Three original water-wheels - one can be seen on the left - were replaced by sluices but much nineteenth-century machinery remains intact and is demonstrated on certain days.

It is commendable that the Trust should have acquired good examples of water-mills, wind pumps and windmills, since so many of these once essential contributors to the country's economy have become ruinous or disappeared altogether. Part of Houghton Mill is now in use as a Youth Hostel.

CHIPPING CAMPDEN MARKET HALL
Gloucestershire

THE MARKET HALL. HIGH ST. CAMPDEN. C37.

It is a pity the photographer chose a time when a normally busy street was deserted before taking his picture. Owning comparatively few town properties, views of Trust properties are seldom animated by period transport or other street activity. This scene, however, does rather emphasise the state of the roadway itself in the era of horse traffic. In light-hearted moments card collectors have competed for the dirtiest Edwardian street and it is a fact that the significance of the horse in daily life at this time is often overlooked.

In *Victorian England: The Horsedrawn Society*, F.M.L. Thompson has calculated that in 1902, three and a half million horses in Britain ate an average of 6 tons of food per year, the product of 4 to 5 acres of land, and provided an estimated 10 million tons of horse droppings annually.

The card shows the gabled Jacobean market house gracing a High Street little changed since it was issued. Remove signs and cover parking lines and a period film set can soon be created which is what was done when making *The Canterbury Tales*. Campden's prefix 'Chipping' has associations with early trading and markets, derived from the Anglo-Saxon word *ceap*, a purchase or bargain, and the source of such words as 'cheap' and 'chapman', a pedlar.

WADDESDON MANOR STABLES
Buckinghamshire

THE STABLES, WADDESDON MANOR.

In a horse-oriented society stables formed a vital part of every country house complex, providing the animals for everyday transport and for hunting. It was often well into the twentieth century before the coach-house became the motor house, the word *garage* only gradually coming into use later.

Stables at National Trust properties have been converted for a wide variety of uses apart from adaptation as residences, restaurants, shops, mothers' rooms or exhibition areas. The surviving stables at Clumber provide Trust Regional Offices; those at Penrhyn Castle house a collection of industrial locomotives. Charlecote and Arlington Court are among those retaining old associations with displays of coaches; at Wimpole Hall there is a full Victorian restoration with heavy horses still occupying the stalls. Robert Adam worked on the massive stable block at Nostell Priory and for early publishers such scenes were often of sufficient interest or architectural quality to serve as a postcard subject.

Here at Waddesdon the stables were designed by Destailleur, the architect who built the house, and were completed in 1884. They now accommodate the restaurant and shop. The bronze statue of a horse which can be seen in the courtyard was the work of J.E. Boehm, sculptor of the Duke of Wellington's monument at Hyde Park Corner.

SPEKE HALL
Merseyside

One of the most richly timbered sixteenth-century houses in the country now stands nearly alongside Liverpool airport. Also an anachronism is this 1907 postcard. There was then a craze for cards manufactured from unusual materials and one surprising choice was aluminium. These cards required a penny stamp instead of the usual halfpenny one but they soon attracted Post Office disapproval as it was claimed that they damaged both other mail and postmen's fingers. Such cards were then obliged to carry as an instruction: 'This card *must* be sent under cover only.' Much of the novelty in sending them was then lost so an enterprising publisher came up with an effective imitation, the 'Alumino' postcard, silvered to look like aluminium, of which this is an example.

The rural neighbourhood of Speke until well into this century emerges from the visitors' booklet issued for the Bass Brewery Excursion from Burton-on-Trent to Liverpool in 1908: 'Our train whirls us by Halewood, a pleasant old-fashioned hamlet embosomed in trees, with thatched cottages and houses of the black and white style as shown in our view of nearby Speke Hall.'

HAM HOUSE
Surrey

SURREY EDUCATION COMMITTEE.

HAM HOUSE.

E.S.A. LONDON. *Copyright.*

Never Absent, Never Late *10/3/05.*

Early in the century a number of Education Committees and County Councils gave away picture postcards commending school pupils for good work or regular attendance. Some commercial firms joined in with sets of cards that also included discreet advertising. Designs were naturally of an educational nature, often of local or famous national landmarks, as with Surrey, Hampshire and Huddersfield.

Various nature series were featured by Isle of Ely Education Committee and for Cadbury's sets of cards; Oxfordshire pictured British wild flowers. Sometimes the category of the reward, such as 'Good Work' or 'French Sentences', and the name of child and school were added.

Many cards, like this unknown pupil's 'Never Absent, Never Late' reward, were proudly preserved in family postcard albums. This recipient could hardly have surmised that a time would come when school parties would actually be conducted round Ham House on educational visits for here, today, is a remarkable survival, little altered, of an original Baroque great house with its restored seventeenth-century formal garden.

RILEY GRAVES, EYAM
Derbyshire

Riley Graves, Eyam

O ne of the more unusual Trust properties is this sad little enclosure on a peaceful Derbyshire hillside.

The story of the inhabitants of Eyam during the plague of 1665-6 is well known and there is much of interest to see and visit in Eyam itself, but this scene recalls the tragedy of one family, the Hancocks. Over the eight days from the 3rd to the 10th of August, 1665, the mother saw her husband and six children die. They were buried in the Righ Lea, an eight-acre meadow, from which the present name of the graves is derived. The tomb of the father, John Hancock, is in its original place, the other stones having been brought together from around the field to form this little circle of six headstones surrounding the father's resting place.

On the last Sunday in August a commemoration service is still held in nearby Cucklet Dell where the Rev. Mompesson, the heroic rector of Eyam, held outdoor services for his dwindling flock throughout the dreadful visitation. The card dates from 1905. The site was given to the Trust in 1939.

THE NEEDLES
Isle of Wight

Edwardian postcard photographers have left us an enormous legacy of contemporary scenes and there are few places where they did not penetrate, often travelling on foot or by bicycle, lumbered with cumbersome cameras, plates and equipment. This photograph has involved a boat trip and offers a scene that seems unchanging but even within the last two hundred years considerable alterations have taken place and erosion is still occurring.

The original 'needle' was a tall, thin pinnacle, 120 feet high, which toppled in 1764. At that time the 'needles' were still connected, the sea breaking through in the early nineteenth century. There was formerly a lighthouse on the great headland above but the site became a fort in 1861 and this has now been restored by the National Trust with a history of this famous feature displayed in the old powder magazine.

THE BRIDGE HOUSE, AMBLESIDE
Cumbria

In 1926 this unusual property was bought by local subscription and handed over to the National Trust to become its first information and recruitment centre. The card precedes that event and is much travelled, having been returned to England from Canada with a message saying: 'You told me you would enjoy seeing some of my post-cards of England. I bought this when you were a baby.'

The Bridge House stands in the middle of Ambleside over Stock Ghyll and dates from the mid-seventeenth century. It was associated with Ambleside Hall and was possibly used originally as a store or summer-house. When disposed of, it served a variety of purposes - pigeon house, weaving shop, teahouse and a cobbler's workroom, while a family with six children is recorded as having lived in it in the 1840s. The upstairs room is reached only by the outside staircase.

CROSTHWAITE CHURCH
Cumbria

Crosthwaite, the old Parish Church of Keswick , is not, of course, a National Trust property but it qualifies for inclusion in this collection. Its vicar from 1883 until 1917 was Canon H.D. Rawnsley, co-founder with Octavia Hill and Sir Robert Hunter of the National Trust and Honorary Secretary from 1895 until his death in 1920. A prodigious worker for the cause of conservation, particularly in the Lake District, Canon Rawnsley was also a writer, lecturer and active participant in many other spheres. He and his first wife, Edith, are buried in the churchyard and there is a memorial to Canon Rawnsley's achievement during his long period as vicar. The tomb of the poet Robert Southey is also here.

Interesting and beautiful within, the church is surrounded by an equal beauty without - the scenery that Canon Rawnsley loved and towards the preservation of which he played so notable a part. His Trust memorial is Friar's Crag and Lord's Island on nearby Derwentwater, bought by public subscription in 1922.

HEVENINGHAM HALL
Suffolk

Heveningham Hall

Another curiosity earning a place in a National Trust postcard collection - a house that was once administered by the Trust but never became a Trust property. A fine Georgian mansion of 1779 with the exterior by Sir Robert Taylor, the interior and an orangery by James Wyatt, and park and gardens by 'Capability' Brown, Heveningham was purchased by the government in 1970 to secure preservation of the hall and its contents, and offered to the Trust. No endowment was forthcoming, however. Rather reluctantly the Trust agreed to administer the property on behalf of the Department of the Environment, while the Government sought to re-sell privately.

This period of agency is unique in England although in Northern Ireland such management of properties has been practised - again, not without difficulties. At Heveningham the unsuitability of agency administration led to the Trust terminating the temporary arrangements in 1980.

MOW COP
Cheshire/Staffordshire borders

MOW COP, CAMP MEETING OFFICIALS.

Hardly the sort of group today's visitors would expect to meet on these rugged slopes rising nearly 1100 feet above sea level to a mock Gothic folly of 1750. Contrasting with a purely decorative and artificial monument, this place was the scene, on a May Sunday in 1807, of the birth of Primitive Methodism. A camp meeting convened by Hugh Bourne and lasting for fourteen hours called for a return to plainer and simpler forms of worship.

Many camp meetings followed, the card showing leaders at the centenary camp of 1907. The Methodist Church was reunited in 1932 but because of the site's significance, 10,000 people gathered here again in 1937, surely the largest crowd ever to assemble for the handing-over of a property to the National Trust.

"HANBURY HALL"

Before most present-day National Trust properties came into their ownership, the names of many notable residences were to be seen emblazoned on the sides of railway locomotives during the heyday of steam.

On the Great Western Railway whole classes of express engines were named after manors, courts, granges, abbeys and castles. With the end of the steam age some property owners acquired the brass nameplates and displayed them, perhaps along with photographs of their 'home' engine as, for instance, at Clevedon Court.

In a Trust postcard collection there would seem to be a place for including such examples. This is 'Hall' class locomotive No. 4931 of the GWR named *Hanbury Hall* (Hereford and Worcester) the attractive red-brick house of 1701 acquired by the Trust in 1953, only a decade before the working days of many of these fine engines were drawing to a close.

A LA RONDE
Devon

As the National Trust acquires additional properties, a search is made for old photographs and postcards which may record past appearances, often invaluable in the renovation generally necessary before a property is reopened to the public. This unusual house came to the Trust in 1990 and is, in effect, sixteen-sided, with 20 rooms radiating around a high octagonal central hall.

1991 saw the acquisition of Chastleton House, Oxfordshire, with which many people became familiar through the B.B.C. television series, *Scoop*, made in 1986 and featuring this delightful and little altered Jacobean manor house under the name *Boot Magna*.

Bibliography

B. Bailey, *English Manor Houses* (Robert Hale 1983)

P.E. Baughan, *Vol. II, North and Mid-Wales - A Regional History of the Railways of Great Britain* (David and Charles 1980)

N. Burton, *The Historic Houses Handbook* (Macmillan)

D.N. Durant, *Living in the Past* (Aurum Press1988)

R. Fedden, *The Continuing Purpose* (Longmans 1968)

J. Franklin, *The Gentleman's Country House and its Plans* (Routledge and Kegan Paul 1981)

J. Gaze, *Figures in a Landscape* (Barrie and Jenkins 1988)

L. Greaves and M. Trinnick, *The National Trust Guide* (The National Trust 1989)

C.W. Hill, *Discovering Picture Postcards* (Shire Publications Ltd 1970)

T. and V. Holt. *Picture Postcards of the Golden Age* (Postcard Publishing Company 1978)

C. Hussey and J. Cornforth, *English Country Houses Open the Public, fourth edition* (Country Life Ltd. 1964)

A.J. Lambert, *Country House Life from Old Photographs* (Batsford 1981)

J. Lees-Milne, *Ancestral Voices* (Chatto and Windus Ltd. 1975)

R. Lewis, '*Kinver Rock Houses,*' Picture Postcard Monthly, No.143 (March 1991)

G. Murphy, *Founders of the National Trust* (Christopher Helm 1987)

V. Sackville-West, *Knole and the Sackvilles* (The National Trust 1991)

C.S. Sykes, *Country House Album* (Pavilion/Books Ltd 1989)

G.S. Thomas, *Gardens of the National Trust* (Weidenfeld and Nicolson)

A. Tinniswood, *Historic Houses of the National Trust* (The National Trust 1991)

R. Turner, *The Smaller English House - 1500-1939* (Batsford 1952)

The National Trust Handbook

Properties of the National Trust

Individual Guide Books to National Trust Properties

Index of National Trust Properties

Those in capital letters feature with picture and text. Other properties mentioned in the text indicated.

A National Trust Old Postcard Album